Tom and Irma

Memories of the 1950s

Susan Patterson

STRATTON
—**PRESS**—
Publishing Life

Tom and Irma
Copyright © 2021 **Susan Patterson**

Stratton Press Publishing
831 N Tatnall Street Suite M #188,
Wilmington, DE 19801
www.stratton-press.com
1-888-323-7009

ISBN (Paperback): 978-1-64895-440-5
ISBN (Ebook): 978-1-64895-441-2

Printed in the United States of America

For my parents,
Tom and Irma

Preface

THIS BOOK WAS AN UNPLANNED project. The *Tom and Irma* chronicles began when I was asked to write a commentary feature for *Radio Kinver*, an international podcast originating from England. It was then that I wrote the first memory piece of my parents, Tom and Irma Traise. From this initial request, listener enthusiasm grew, one story begat another, then another, and to my surprise, the reflections that I thought so inconsequential and ordinary spoke to people all over the world. Tom and Irma had fans.

The chapters in this book are individual glimpses of life in America in the 1950s. Tom and Irma Traise are the main characters. Collectively, the episodes are a combination of lessons that can speak to us in different ways and with different force. We all come to understand life at a variety times and for a myriad of reasons. Sometimes that understanding has a price; sometimes it is free. Tom and

Irma provided the opportunity for understanding and learning, and it was, and still is, free.

My hope is that you will savor these reflections of Tom and Irma and that each of you will find a Tom and Irma somewhere in your life.

Prologue

WHAT YOU ARE ABOUT TO read are stories of life during the 1950s in a small town in the state of Oregon of the United States of America. They are based on my memories of my parents, Tom and Irma Traise, and their three children: Richard, Sharon, and Susan. The accounts are true, and the humor, happiness, sadness, love, and lives were real.

Prologue

Contents

CHAPTER
One

Ours Is to be Like Tom and Irma

My parents, Tom and Irma Traise, lived in Molalla, Oregon in the 1950s with their three children. It was a good time in the world. There was hope even though World Wars I and II had ravaged much of the world. And like millions of other families looking toward a peaceful and prosperous future, our family was full of hope as well.

I hardly read the newspapers or listen to the television news anymore. I used to. I used to read almost the whole paper and be very current with the latest news, especially that of a political nature. Now I am taking a bit of a rest. I am insulating myself from the dead of war and the living horrors of our world. I know that this is a dangerous dodge of reality, but that's what I am doing—for a little while anyway.

Indulge me if you will, however, to talk for a bit about something else. I would like to tell you about my parents. They were Tom and Irma Traise, born in 1909 and 1912 respectively. My father's family came from Cornwall, England. We don't know from where my mother's family hailed, but as the story goes, Mom's father was quite the scallywag and ran illegal liquor over the Canadian border. Neither Dad nor Mom was well educated, but both were extremely bright.

My father was a logger. He quit school at the age of fourteen and went to work in the logging camps in the Upper Peninsula of Michigan. Tom could tell you how many board feet were in a tree just by looking at it. He could run his finger down a column of two- or three-digit numbers and add them instantly as his fingers moved down the column. And he could play any instrument he picked up.

My mother worked taking care of people all of her life. She came from pretty rough circumstances, and she survived by taking care of others. Irma nursed people and cleaned for them and befriended them. She also was a wonderful cook, and she too learned her craft in the logging camps. She cooked for hundreds of sturdy hard-living men who burned off more calories before 10:00 a.m. than most people eat in a whole day. People depended upon Irma. She knew what they needed. She was a good friend to many during her life journey.

Tom and Irma always, always tried to do the right thing. That's what I learned from them. They would stop and offer to help someone broken down on the highway. They took in strays. They donated to the veterans. They bought encyclopedias for their children. They didn't sue anyone. They didn't fight. Tom and Irma did nothing great in this world. Just a whole bunch of good little things.

But now, back to today. Poverty, floods, famine, hatred, wars. What to do? There are people working all over the earth to make this world better for the millions who suffer from the ravages of human weakness and nature's might. Throughout history, many have donated huge amounts of time or money to just and good causes. I am so impressed and humbled by those who make big differences.

Most of us cannot make big and bold differences in this world. Ours is to be like Tom and Irma. Making small differences in our own small worlds. Any number of unknown small efforts can change the universe. I'm counting on that. I'm counting that Tom and Irma's lives made an impact.

There is so much that we do wrong in this world. Some say it is because of incarnate sin. Some say it is because of stupidity. Probably it is a little of both. However, I believe that we are better today, not worse than yesterday, and better yet to be. Yes, we do make mistakes, but we do get things right sometimes as well. It is the little things that made a difference for me as a child. I am sure that they did not know it, but Tom and Irma made the world better a little bit at a time.

CHAPTER
Two

One Cannot Deny Progeny

MY PARENTS, TOM AND IRMA Traise, lived in Molalla, Oregon in the 1950s with their three children. Americans wanted a better world. Tom and Irma were no different. They wanted more for their children than they had in their childhood. I think about them often, parents who went away so long ago. I'm not quite sure what all they taught me in our short time together, but I know it was significant. Most of it was subliminal, and only now I am realizing where my ethics and habits came from.

I was a favored child, the youngest of three. There were seven years between each of us siblings, and each time my mother was pregnant, she was told she could have no more children. My parents were forty and thirty-seven when I was born. Nothing to think about now, but sixty-some years ago, that was fairly old to have children. They were tired, I think, when they raised me. I must have sensed that because I always wanted to be good and to please them.

But now I want to discuss what Tom and Irma taught me. They trained me to try very hard in school, to sit up front in class, to ask for extra credit, to study hard before tests, to ask how to get A's. They told this shy girl to step up and volunteer to play the accordion at the Hawaiian musical presentation. I was given accordion lessons. Yes, accordion. Not the piano, the accordion. Can you imagine this buck-toothed skinny little girl with braids and a huge accordion strapped to her flat chest? Goodness, I was the apple of their eye. Mom and Dad decided that the accordion, unlike the piano, was portable and that I could take it to parties and play for people. You know, I never, never did that. Nope, not once. But I practiced every night while my father watched and listened. My sister did the dishes.

These scholarly habits were implanted by verbally telling me what to do. But there was so much more that they taught me by their unspoken words. Work, for example. They modeled an amazing capacity to work hard. It was a Depression Era thing for them. As I mentioned, Tom was a logger. He drove Cat (to be more specific, it was a Caterpillar Bulldozer 10, and that was a big machine then). He never missed a day's work in the time that he lived.

My mother worked at the cannery on the night shift and took care of elderly people during the day. I went with her on the trips when she cooked for Jack and Ida Wright and for Charlie and Ethel Albright. By the way, Charlie Albright's grandfather clock sits in my dining room today, and one of his wool blankets keeps me warm while I watch television.

There were some difficult times in 1963. That year, my mother went to my junior high school and got me my first job. She didn't ask me what I thought about the subject of working; she just got me the job. That summer I scraped gum off chairs and washed walls at the school. I was fourteen, but it didn't occur to me to complain. I liked the money. I've worked ever since. I still like the money.

Tom and Irma illustrated to us how to get along with other people. They laughed and never fought. They had no enemies, and everyone liked them. They were highly respected in their world. Mom spoke for Dad most of the time, but I knew that they were in agreement in their worldview. I had respect for them as well. Now, let me tell you, these parents of mine weren't perfect. They had their prejudices. Their biased ideas, I think, were also typical of the Depression generation. However, I believe that their narrow-mindedness was not that of decision, but of beliefs born from a lack of knowledge and understanding. I shudder to think what people of a different skin color or what gay people would say if they heard how my mother talked then! But still and all, through their demonstration of a myriad of kindnesses, their enduring friendships, and their love for each other, Mom and Dad modeled for me how to live in what I hope to be a kindly, intelligent, and accepting manner.

Tom and Irma also taught me not to give up. They didn't. My parents planned and tried this and that. On the surface, nothing seemed to work out. But underneath, who knows the number of people they helped or how many seeds they planted. They didn't ever stop trying. Each was working on the day he and she died. If their lives were measured by the typical American standard of how much education one has, the type of house one lives in, or how much money one leaves behind, then they would not have been deemed successful. But if we measure by other means, if we count what was taught to one little girl who came later in life, then there was huge achievement. They may not have been successful by the American standard, but I am. I am, and therefore, they were too. One cannot deny progeny. My good fortune is theirs. But you know, Tom and Irma were no different from any other parents. Your parents were the same type of honest, hardworking people. Your mom and dad taught you good things, and they helped you to become the good person you are today. That's the point of parenting. Tom and Irma were not unlike a lot of other parents; they were just my parents.

CHAPTER
Three

I Want to Drive a Packard

My parents, Tom and Irma Traise, lived in Molalla, Oregon in the 1950s with their three children. America was becoming a world leader in the auto industry. Cars by then were a vital part of everyday life. During that time, Tom and Irma owned a 1954 Packard Clipper Deluxe, license plate 9E 1725. The car was a beautiful machine that was dependable and sure. The Packard was big, heavy, and it had power. Even as a young girl, I could sense its strength and stability. I'm pretty sure that my parents did not buy it new, but I remember that it was a very nice car nevertheless. One year my dad decided he did not like the green color and painted it black. I don't know, I liked the old green color. But then I was just a young girl.

I got to sit up front most of the time with them on that long bench seat that had plenty of room. I would usually get carsick in the back seat. My dad smoked unfiltered Camel cigarettes, creating a considerable amount of secondhand smoke that swirled around in the car. It probably contributed to my motion sickness more than anything, but we didn't know about all of the dangers of cigarettes in the 1950s. I just got to sit up front.

Tom drove most of the time. My mother was quite capable, but Dad did the driving. In my mother's eyes, that was not good. Even though Tom was the best driver in the woods, where he worked, on the open road, he caused problems. He drove slowly—very, very slowly. We always had a line of cars behind us. Sometimes honking. Oh, the embarrassment. Mom would tell him to hurry up. My sister would tell him to drive faster. I would say nothing. It didn't matter anyway. Tom would drive exactly how he wanted to. He knew his pace. So there you were, this man dressed up, wearing a fedora tilted to one side, a Camel cigarette clenched between his teeth, three female passengers in the car, steering the Packard down the highway with a long trail of frustrated drivers behind him. Oh my goodness. Today he would be the cause of major road rage.

My parents were responsible and respectful people. They did things right. My dad would go out long before it was time to leave and warm up the Packard. I think that's what one needed to do back then. We always left in plenty of time, just in case we got a flat tire. As far as I remember, we never had a flat tire, and we always arrived early at our destination. (By the way, my husband and I leave way ahead of time as well. We are hurry-up-and-wait type of people.)

Oregon had a lot of snow in those days. And don't forget, my parents were from the Upper Peninsula of Michigan and were used to much more snow than Oregonians ever thought of. They also knew the value of respecting the weather. Tom and Irma were always prepared…just in case something happened. To get home to Molalla, we often had to maneuver up three long steep hills in the neighboring town of Oregon City. In my heart, I knew that it wasn't a problem, but my mom and dad would discuss the process of snow driving, getting home, and whether or not they needed to put chains on the tires.

I remember one winter when it was particularly bad. We were at the bottom of Washington Street in Oregon City. And it was real slick. There were cars sliding and getting stuck all over the place. One lone car was working its way up the hill. I remember my dad saying, "We'll wait and let him get up the hill, and then we will give 'er a try." There it was again. Respect. Tom didn't try to pass the less-experienced snow driver on the right or get around him on the left. He didn't drive close up behind the car that was trying to make it the best it could. He gave the driver space. Tom didn't yell or swear or get impatient. He knew he would make it when his turn came. (Dad was, after all, driving a Packard, and he knew how to get machines almost anywhere, albeit slowly.) But that's just it. Then, drivers took turns. They stopped at yellow lights. They acknowledged each other. They recognized the importance and privilege of driving an automobile. There was respect on the road.

My mom started teaching me how to drive as soon as it was legal. She didn't mess around. The day after I turned fifteen, she took me down to get my driving permit, and one year later, I got my license. Unlike Tom, Irma drove fast. So that is what she taught me.

"Watch and get ready to go when the light turns green. Get off the line ahead of the other cars!"

"What are you waiting for, an engraved invitation?"

"Pass those cars!"

That was Mom. Well, I'm here to tell you that I've never had a car accident, so somewhere between Dad and Mom and my guardian angel, I've made it thus far. I must say that learning two different perspectives of road management has certainly influenced my life in odd but effective ways.

These days, I drive much more slowly than I used to. I've learned my father's pace. It suits me now. Oh, make no mistake, I move right along on the freeway and in the fast lane. But about four years ago, I made a conscious decision to slow down. I like it better. I enjoy the scenery more. On our country roads, I drive right down the middle of two lanes, sometimes with impatient people behind me. They can't pass. I'm driving down the middle of the road. It's only a mile that I do this, so no one is too put out…I hope.

My parents taught me a great deal by simply driving a car. Whether it was respect for time, autos, other drivers, the elements, or their own abilities, they paid attention. I do so want to be respectful as well. I hope that I am. I want to give people space. I want to let them try to make it, and then I'll try. I want to slow down and enjoy the road. I want to wave at people and smile. I want to drive a Packard.

CHAPTER
Four

Canasta Camaraderie

My parents, Tom and Irma Traise, lived in Molalla, Oregon in the 1950s with their three children. America was relaxing after decades of poverty and war. Even though McCarthyism and the Cold War hovered in the background, enjoyment was a lifestyle for its people.

In those years, Tom and Irma often played the card game canasta with Harley and Dorothy Crockett. Harley Crockett was the union boss, a very important man in our small town. Mr. Crockett represented the workers of the Weyerhaeuser Timber Company where my dad was employed. Harley was a big man of presence. He was not threatening at all, but you knew that he could take care of the workers well and negotiate a hard bargain when he needed to.

Dorothy Crockett, I thought, was very sophisticated. She had black curly hair, talked very fast, and wore fashionable clothing, including toreador pants. She probably did not have the shape to wear such clothes, but in those years, I don't think women worried about their figures as much as we do now. The Crockets had a daughter, Nancy, and a son, Jimmy. Jimmy was out of the house when we socialized with the family. Nancy and my sister, Sharon, were about the same age and passed the time with each other while our parents were shuffling, dealing, and trading the gossip of a small town. I, for the most part, kept quiet and watched all that was going on.

As a contrast to that simple time in our modern history, canasta was a very complicated card game to understand, and yet, it was wildly popular. I remember that it involved lots of cards, red threes were important, there were naturals, piles got frozen, there were dirty canastas, you could go out…and, well, that's about all I can come up with now. We did play canasta together as a family as well. I absolutely loved playing cards, and I always worked it so that I was my dad's partner. I must have been around eight or nine in the card-playing frenzy years. I remember that I could hardly hold all those cards in my hands, but in my mind, I strategized and played with the best of them. Mom and Dad could always tell when I had a good hand. I would have a determined, focused look in my eyes and have a ton of cards to hold between my small fingers. There would be so many, in fact, that I had to stack them on the table in front of me. I was always planning a big move with all those cards.

Tom and Irma and Harley and Dorothy were serious card players. They would go until one or two in the morning, with Mom always promising me we that would go home after one more hand. I learned that my mother was just putting me off with those empty promises, but I found ways to entertain myself and eventually fell asleep on Dorothy's couch.

Most of the time I wandered around Crocketts' house. I thought it was ever so much better than ours. Dorothy had maroon and pink tile in the bathroom and very ornate knobs on the doors. There was turquoise linoleum in the kitchen, and everything was very clean and free of clutter. A bit unlike our house, I must say, although we did have maroon and gray paneling in our dining room. (With regard to that maroon and gray paneling, there was a little story behind it. My dad was always remodeling or fixing something. When it came time to redo the dining room, Tom suggested the colored paneling. My mom thought it would be a horrible idea and campaigned vigorously against it. She, however, eventually gave in, still doubting the design capability of Tom. Well, Dad was right. The colored panels were beautiful. Everyone commented about them, and Mom had a story to tell about trusting Dad. We talked about that little project for years.)

I don't know, but maybe entertainment in general was different then. It was nothing for a family to go for a car ride on Sunday and drive out to see if, for example, Walter and Emily Spurgeon and the six Spurgeon offspring were home. Well, what were you supposed to do? Drive by, see that they were at home, and then keep going? No. You stopped in to say hello. People dropped by on Sundays. My parents had us girls convinced that Dad could always tell when someone was coming over. We would hurry and clean up the house, just on the chance that someone might come by on Sunday afternoon. I don't think that people go visiting on Sundays anymore. I don't know, but no one ever drops by our house on Sundays anyway. But my house is usually clean on Sundays, just in case.

One Sunday afternoon, my parents were visiting Walter and Dorothy Warren. Walter worked in the woods with my dad. In fact, Walter and Dorothy were the ones who talked Mom and Dad into moving from Michigan to Oregon. On that particular afternoon, the Traises and the Warrens were having a very nice visit indeed. I was, of course, entertaining myself quietly, all the while listening to the adult conversation. They were at the kitchen table, and my mom, not wanting to overstay, said something like "Well, Tom, we'd better be going home now." My dad responded quite loudly, "Irma, we can't go, Dorothy hasn't even offered us any coffee yet!" Everyone laughed. (Humor was simple then as well.) My mother was mortified. I don't know why. Dorothy responded with coffee and chocolate cake, and eventually, Dad let us know when it was time to go. Such was the leisure life for a small family from a small town in America in the 1950s.

I struggled in writing this piece. I was all over the board with remnants of my life's fabric here and there. Dots and spots of happenings and people. Recollections of happy that shuttered the sad. But nothing fit together. What was the point of my ramblings? I kept asking myself. What was I trying to say? Well, maybe that was it. Maybe there didn't need to be a point. Happy memories, even short ones, are good.

CHAPTER
Five

We Never Had a Babysitter

MY PARENTS, TOM AND IRMA Traise, lived in Molalla, Oregon in the 1950s with their three children. A great evil had been vanquished in the world, and optimism was everywhere. General Eisenhower was now President Eisenhower, and he was just as good in peacetime as he was in war. We looked on the sunny side of life.

Mom and Dad were encouraging parents. Even though I assume there was not a lot of money in the household, we were given the needs and wants of new outfits for every holiday and special occasion, lessons if we wanted them, and the general backup that most parents give, but that their children often do not understand until much later in life. It was not unusual for my parents to help their children in complicated, possibly hair-brained, and not always successful situations.

I remember one year my sister Sharon was going to some affair at the high school. She wanted an umbrella dress. It was apparently the rage. Even though my mother had no clue how to make the umbrella dress, Irma got into the drama of the idea. Mom planned and sewed and tried this and that, and we were all very excited. I remember Sharon trying on the dress many times. It was a gorgeous off-the-shoulder emerald green taffeta piece that flowed to just below the knee, and then the whole thing swooped under like an upside down umbrella…or open umbrella or right-side-up umbrella. I never really understood the comparison. Sharon had lots of stunning dark auburn hair, a lovely figure, and a beautiful dark complexion. The dress was perfect for her. Now, I was quite a bit younger than my sister and wasn't interested in beautiful dresses, but I enjoyed in the hoopla, nevertheless. I don't even know if my sister had a date for the dance, but thank god, she had the dress.

After he came home from the army in 1957, my brother Dick became interested in skin diving. As a family, we would all pile into the car and drive up to Hood Canal in Washington State and do whatever to pass the time, while Dick explored the undersea wilderness of the Pacific Northwest. At one point, Dick thought it would be a great idea to make skin diving flags that attached to a buoy and marked where a diver was swimming underwater. The plan was to sell the flags to diving shops, and Dick would make lots of money. My mother took to the sewing machine again. She made skin diving flags to beat the band. I remember putting them in plastic packages for the shops. We had dozens of white and red diving flags all over the living room. I don't think they sold well, but again, my parents supported whatever their children tried.

But here is the deal. They would back us even when we didn't try. One summer when I was about eight years old, a man came to town and announced that he would be offering swimming lessons to all the children. Of course, my folks asked me if I wanted to learn to swim. I said sure. So one Saturday, we all went to the public pool where the instructor (who talked fast and loud and whom I did not take to very well) was shouting directions to everyone. All of us young children were lined up in the water along the sides of the pool. All of the parents were watching beside the pool.

There I was, a skinny little girl, shivering, with a bunch of people staring and listening to a man I didn't like, who was yelling orders. We children were standing there waiting for instructions. The man yelled, "Okay, everybody get down under the water and make bubbles!" *What! How?* I thought. All the kids did what he said. I did not. Then he saw me. He kept yelling, "Get down!" and waving his arms downward, motioning that I should be under the water. I just stood there. I don't know how long I was standing while all the other kids were learning to swim. It was all a blur. Eventually I got out. My parents wrapped a towel around me. The swimming instructor barked that I was not ready. My mother cooed that I was not ready. It wasn't that I wasn't ready; I didn't even try!

But you know, it didn't seem to matter how good we were at things or what crazy ideas we had. They loved us and cared about us. Whatever we children were interested in, they were interested in. We never had a babysitter. Tom and Irma were always home with us in the evenings. When we went somewhere, usually Mom or Dad was pretty darn close. At the very least, they always knew where we were.

Mom and Dad taught us what they knew and how to live an honest and good life. My brother and sister and I went our separate ways. But we each took much of Tom and Irma along with us. They don't know we did, Tom and Irma. They don't know how we turned out or what we are doing now. But I do things now how I think my parents would want me to do them. I remember. I know that their lessons and interest and involvement meant something important when I was a child, and it still does now.

CHAPTER
Six

Elizabeth

My parents, Tom and Irma Traise, lived in Molalla, Oregon in the 1950s with their three children. It was an easy time. Childhood was simple. My family was not wealthy or sophisticated, but we were kindly and, because of my mother, generally civilized. I was the youngest of the three children, and there was seven years difference between each of us. Because of the age difference, my siblings weren't playmates, but that was all right because I found other friends to play with. I am going to tell you about one of my friends now.

As with most of you, I had a dog. Her name was Elizabeth. We called her Lizzy. She was given to me as a present one year for my birthday. Elizabeth was a black-and-white cocker spaniel, and she was a cutie. She was smart and devoted, and my dad taught her some tricks. She could sit and beg, which she did at mealtime, much to my mother's dismay. Actually, it really annoyed all of us, but we couldn't seem to untrain her from begging, and she did get a little plump over the years. Daddy would cut her hair in the summer, and she looked like something out of the Disney movie *Lady and the Tramp*, with her big long eyelashes and short curly hair all over her sausage body.

Elizabeth was well mannered and a good sport about several things. Now, as I mentioned, Lizzy was a bit chubby; I was small. I think that we were about the same weight. One year, Dad made me a play area in a grove of trees on our property. Among the big climbing trees, there was a swing, a gymnastics bar, and a teeter-totter. To make play more fun, Dad put a wooden box on one end of the teeter-totter for Lizzy. I would naturally sit on the other end. She would teeter with me only for a little while, and then would get bored and jump off. But she did it. She was a good friend to me.

Early in Elizabeth's life, my dad built a harness and a cart for her. I would put my doll in the cart, and Elizabeth would pull it down the road. My parents thought this was very smart indeed. They suggested that I would like to be in the Fourth of July parade. Now this was not an ordinary parade, mind you. It was a big deal. People came from miles around to watch it. It was quite long because there were so many participants who marched in it. There were, of course, a slew of horses, but also cars, logging trucks, clowns and/or politicians, marching bands, and just about anything or anyone else you could possibly think of. But even at a young age, Lizzy and I were up for it. I had her on a leash, and she pulled the cart along with my doll in it. I don't know if people were impressed, but I had a grand time. For a quiet little girl, walking alone in that parade was quite an accomplishment.

My very favorite thing to do with Elizabeth, however, was to go for bike rides with her. My dad, seeing that she was very clever, taught her to ride in the basket of my bicycle. Now keep in mind that my bicycle was not sleek or built for speed or ease of maneuverability. It had fat tires, was small, heavy, and not easy to steer. As an adult dog, Lizzy was probably thirty pounds, which was a lot for me to handle. But I could manage the whole thing pretty well once got going fast enough. And off we would go! There we would be riding around the town, Lizzy's ears flapping back in the wind, and my braids flying back in the wind. I imagine we were a sight. Even in unpretentious little Molalla, that must have looked silly. I am sure that there were snickers behind my back, but I really didn't care what people thought in those years.

My parents persuaded me to be in the Fourth of July parade a second time. I rarely said no to Mom and Dad. The idea was that Lizzy and I would ride in a bicycle built for two. They decked out my bike with streamers and ribbons, they put my mother's apron around poor Lizzy's neck, and I wore a cowboy hat. And there we were in the parade again, me riding my bike with Lizzy in the basket. She was a bit nervous as you can imagine. Walking in a parade was one thing, but being up in the basket of a some-times-wobbly bike was another. The parade was noisy and boisterous. But my mother, who was by that time pushing fifty and a somewhat broad woman, ran along at the side of the street to keep up with us and to make sure that Lizzy stayed in the basket and that I was alright. Lizzy did. We finished. I got a ribbon. Everyone was thrilled. I'm sure that my mom was near exhaustion after that little aerobic adventure, but she was, as ever, proud of me.

Like most dogs, Elizabeth loved to ride in the car. Often, as my dad drove our Packard, she would ride on the top of the bench seat behind my dad's shoulder. She would balance her broad body there, steadied by my dad's back. Of course, Lizzy loved to look out of the open window from that position and would often lean out as far as she could. One day, she leaned out so far that she fell out of the car. Now keep in mind, my dad did not drive fast, so I doubt that in downtown Molalla where Elizabeth fell out, she hurt herself. My dad didn't even notice that she was gone until he got home. How that happened, I don't know. You would think that he would have noticed a fat dog missing off his shoulder! But when he did figure out that he didn't have my dog, he immediately went back downtown to fetch her. And there she was, sitting on the corner, just waiting for him. He stopped the car, opened the door, invited her to get in, and she did. No harm, no foul. As I mentioned, Lizzy was a good sport.

I think that everyone should have had a dog named Elizabeth or Charley or Buster or Roxie. I believe that it would be a simple solution to many of our human problems. There are probably an abundance of simple solutions. I am convinced that it is the simple things that one starts out with in life that makes the big differences so many years later in life.

CHAPTER
Seven

Fishing, Fast Cars, and Fudgesicles

My parents, Tom and Irma Traise, lived in Molalla, Oregon in the 1950s with their three children. Americans could abandon themselves to flourishing, and fear was not a big part of our day-to-day concerns. My brother Richard—or Dick, as we called him then—was fourteen years older than I, and in 1957, he was just returning from his tour of duty in the army. For some reason or another, he took a special interest in me. It might have been because there were so many deaths in our family in the ten-month period before I was born, or it might have been that I was just an odd little duckling, and he took pity on me. Either way, Dick and I sure had a lot of fun doing things that today would have gotten us into a lot of trouble.

Dick was an outdoorsman. He liked fishing and hunting and tromping around in the woods. In Molalla, our small little logging town, one only had to go a few miles to find woods aplenty. And much to my enjoyment, Dick often took me with him on his outdoor excursions. He bought a red three-wheeled Harley-Davidson motorcycle that had a trunk type of thing on the back. I would sit on the trunk lid and hold on to the handles of that trunk for dear life as Dick drove down the road. That bike was a fine piece of machinery, and we would ride all over the Molalla countryside on it. We would go exploring, target shooting, and hiking. We also would do a lot of fishing. Dick bought me a small rod and reel set and a basket filled with lures, sinkers, and other such necessities. I packed and repacked that basket all the time. Dick taught me how to tie knots, stick worms on hooks, and to fish like a semipro. I don't remember catching a lot of fish, but that wasn't the point. My favorite part of a fishing trip was when we would stop at the Y Grocery Store on the way home, and Dick would buy me a ten-cent Nutty Buddy ice cream cone. Once in a while, I would have a Fudgesicle for seven cents.

Here's what the catch was, so to speak, with Dick taking me fishing. He would often come and get me out of school to go for an afternoon of fishing! He would walk up to my elementary teacher and hand her some cock-and-bull story, like there was an emergency and that I was needed at home, or that my mother was in the hospital and he was taking me to visit her, or some other such rubbish. The teacher would actually let me out of school! Can you believe it? I would say nothing and just get up and leave the classroom and go fishing. My parents didn't realize what was going on until it was too late. The truth came out when my teacher saw my mother one time at the grocery store and wondered how she was, since Mom was so sick and in the hospital, according to my brother. My mother put two and two together and just about died of embarrassment. She did see some humor in my brother's antics but, nevertheless, told him to quit taking me out of school. He, for the most part, did.

In addition to the three-wheeled motorcycle that we loved to ride, my brother had a string of cars, from a 1949 Ford to a newer and more stylish Dodge. I remember one time being with Dick when he was driving his Dodge north on Highway 213. Dick asked me if I wanted to go one hundred miles per hour. I, of course, said sure. I watched the speedometer. We did. Dick told me not to tell Mom or Dad. I didn't.

Now, back to my mother. Irma was no shrinking violet. My dad's nickname for her was Irish, if you get what I mean. And Irma knew how to use a butcher knife. Well, let me tell you, there is no doubt in my mind that if my mom ever found out that Dick drove one hundred miles per hour with me in the car, she would have taken after Dick and/or that Dodge with a butcher knife and disabled either one or both of them. She never found out.

We got away with things that were dangerous but, for the most part, harmless in those days. On the other hand, we were watched more closely because there were a lot of people taking care of us children. There were teachers, policemen, firemen, shopkeepers, church people… any adult. And we were taught to respect all of them. They had authority over us. Well, you know, all of those adults in our small town talked to each other too. My sister Sharon didn't get away with as much as Dick did. One time, as a teenage girl might do, she wore short shorts and bright red lipstick in downtown Molalla. Someone who saw Sharon with a group of girls "happened" to drive by our house and told my dad how the girls were dressed. Well, my dad didn't waste any time. He immediately got in the car, went to downtown, and brought Sharon home. No daughter of his would be seen with short shorts or red lipstick in public. Maybe if my sister had said that she was on her way to visit our mother in the hospital, she would have gotten a pass from the tattletale adult.

In that time, there were no drugs, no alcohol, no abuse, no prejudice, no violence, no harm. Well, of course there were. I just didn't know it. My parents protected me. I'm glad they did. I'm a better person for it. I didn't need to know then what kids know now. I learned plenty after I got to be an adult. My childhood was safe. And for that, I am grateful.

CHAPTER
Eight

Irma Lessons

My parents, Tom and Irma Traise, lived in Molalla, Oregon in the 1950s with their three children. American culture was in transition in many ways. The drugs and the anger of the 1960s were not far off, but for the Traises, it was a stable and precious time in our lives. We were homey. There was innocence for a little girl whose parents, especially her mother, protected her.

It was a time when the most scary thing to worry about was the ringer washer, which my mother constantly admonished me to keep my hands away from when she was turning the ringer. I was also warned to keep my hands away from the sewing machine when she was working at it. I still have that machine, and my hands are okay. In hand stitching, Mom could tie a knot perfectly at the end of the thread with one hand every time. I marveled at her ability, but I usually had to thread the needles for her. She said that my younger eyes were better.

It was a time when I would sometimes find wet clothes rolled up in the refrigerator. Mom would sprinkle clothes with water, roll them up, place them in the laundry basket, and then cover them with a towel. When Mom could not quite get the ironing job done, to prevent the clothes from getting moldy, she would put them in the refrigerator to keep them at just the right level of dampness.

It was a time too when I would find cookie dough rolled up in wax paper cooling in the refrigerator or icebox, as we called it. Or there would be bread on the counter rising. Or jars of canned food in the pantry or jars of jelly with wax on top to seal them fresh. Intuitively, my mother was a very good cook. She hardly used a recipe. Mom learned to cook in logging camps; she owned a boarding house, and she made food that was to be eaten with joy. I remember jelly rolls and cakes. Peanut butter fudge, peanut butter cookies, and cinnamon rolls were heaven to me. Pasties, of course, were to please my dad. Back then we did not consider that what we were eating might be bad for us. We just loved the taste. A jar of bacon grease always sat on the stove, ready to be added to many of the dishes that required cooking fat.

The Traises did not entertain a lot. Cocktail parties were not part of our life, but Sunday dinners with guests were. And once in a while, Mother did take time from her busy family schedule to do something grand. One year Mom put on a bridal shower in the form of a mock wedding. "What's a mock wedding?" we asked. She had it all in mind. Irma put on a make-believe wedding. It was a spoof on hillbillies, as she called them. Mother wrote the script, and it was truly funny.

The shower was for Carol Spurgeon, eldest daughter of our good friends, Walter and Emily Spurgeon. We all wore old torn clothes and straw hats. There was a whole made-up hillbilly wedding party. Some poor soul played the bridegroom and was forced with a shotgun to the altar at our house. We all ate and laughed and made fun. I'm sure now that some of what was said would be deemed quite insulting. Good thing I don't remember much of the actual script. But the shower was talked about for years.

Irma was a woman of secrets. There were happenings in her childhood and early adult years that she never spoke of—ever. There were illegal, abusive, and embarrassing experiences that she suffered through. But there wasn't any drama that followed her. Personal lives weren't brought up in the courtroom or splashed all over the newspaper just for the sake of notoriety. Social networking was not the source of exaggeration or absolution. Irma just kept going and didn't talk about such things. She worked and kept on working for a happy home.

Mother held all of her secrets. I suppose she knew that bringing them to light wouldn't help anyone. There was no use dragging her husband and children through the cruel muck of her early life. She just kept moving forward. In recent years, I have put two and two together and figured a few things out. With the answers that I came up with and what relatives have verified, I have found new respect for my mom. I always had admiration for Dad, of course, but Mom just seemed to be another person then. She was not someone to admire necessarily; she was just Mom. I now know differently. I now respect her courage, the can-do attitude she had, and the love she lived for her children. I'm impressed with her ability to have quietly and courageously moved on. Keeping quiet may not always be the best thing to do, but it worked for her, and it might work today for a lot of people who think that telling all is a right and the right thing to do. This might be an Irma lesson from which many could learn.

CHAPTER
Nine

Thomas J. Traise

My parents, Tom and Irma Traise, lived in Molalla, Oregon in the 1950s with their three children. Families were growing. Schools were built. Generations were passing their own knowledge from one to the next. There was time to pay attention to the important things in life.

Each of us children in the Tom Traise family was very different from the other, and there were reasons for that, but I won't go into them right now. I know that my parents didn't prefer one child to the other, but I felt like I was my dad's favorite. Mom seemed to have Dick and Sharon close to her. Daddy had me. Tom Traise was forty years old when I was born. I was somewhat of a surprise to all concerned. In 1942, after my sister was born, my mother was told that she could not have any more children. Seven years after

Sharon, the doctors thought my mother was sick with a tumor. She thought that she was pregnant. Right before the surgery to remove the tumor, the doctors realized my mom was right. I was little and simple and figured out how to behave early on in my life. What middle-aged father would not appreciate such a child? My father was not a large man, so we could often fit side by side in the same chair. He always saved a seat for me.

We entertained each other easily, Daddy and I. I would sit on his lap facing him, and we would play a hand-clapping game, it seemed, for hours. We would clap our hands together and then clap each other's hands in a progressive routine. Then we would keep going faster and faster till one of us would miss. Dad would laugh, and I would want to go again.

Daddy taught me to say, "How much wood could a woodchuck chuck, if a woodchuck could chuck wood? He could chuck as much wood as a woodchuck could, if a woodchuck could chuck wood." Oh, the humor of a logger. There was also the cat's cradle game. We had string, with which we designed patterns around our fingers, and then passed the designs from one to the other. Honestly, you would think a busy, hardworking man would have had more important things to do. Is it possible that Dad defined the important differently than some of us do today? Or maybe he didn't think to define his fatherhood at all. Maybe he just enjoyed it.

Tom also taught me to write my name and to add up numbers. He taught me how to jump over a broomstick while holding it with both hands. He taught me how to knit and to ride a bike and to dance like a Cossack. From carpentry to math to music to companionship, Tom had many abilities and talents that could impress a little girl.

Every week, my father took me to accordion lessons. Every day he sat and listened to me practice. I wasn't any good. He told my mom so, but he still listened to my practices. He did tell me that with his brains and my fingers, we would have one good player. But I didn't have his brains, and without that, my fingers weren't all that useful. I didn't take offense. I didn't particularly like playing the accordion; it was just something that I did.

My dad, Thomas James Traise, was the third of eight children born of Thomas Henry and Emily Garland Traise of Cornwall, England, where they owned a bed-and-breakfast. My grandfather, Thomas Henry Traise, was also a carpenter, and he fought in the Boer War. He lost an eye during battle in Africa. Grandparents Thomas Henry and Emily Garland moved to the US in 1907. They settled in the Upper Peninsula of Michigan in a community of Cornish, Scandinavian, and Italian immigrants. My dad, Thomas James, was born in 1909. All but two of his brothers and sisters died by the early 1920s. Tom was on his own early in life, as most young men were at that time. He quit school at fourteen and went to work. Life wasn't necessarily difficult for the era, but it sure wasn't easy either. Maybe that is why Tom appreciated just one little girl born in 1949.

We all have our various reasons for creating ties that bind. Parents and children are no different. Tom Traise found value in me and I in him. I did not have Tom all that long by comparison to other children and their fathers. But it was enough, and I treasure the time.

Ten

Looking Good, Feeling Even Better

My parents, Tom and Irma Traise, lived in Molalla, Oregon in the 1950s with their three children. Industry was changing and growing in America once again. People were anxious to get on board the new era.

Tom was a logger by trade, but the timber industry in the Upper Peninsula of Michigan was just about down to nothing by the late forties. So for financial reasons, my parents moved to Oregon, along with many other Midwesterners. The Traise family moved to Molalla because friends Dorothy and Walter Warren had already settled there. My dad and my brother drove out first to Oregon, and then my mother, sister, and I followed six months later riding the famous train, the Great Northern Empire Builder, all the way from Michigan. I was three years old, and my first solid memories in this life are of riding that magnificent train.

In the early 1950s of the United States, hope and happiness were in the air. World War II with its horrors was over, and opportunity was everywhere. The US had come through the forties with pride and dignity. Like most people who lived through the Depression Era, Tom and Irma were extraordinary hard workers. Like most Americans, they were happy to be working toward their dreams, and it showed.

Tom and Irma were sharp dressers. Even though they were not rich, both looked pretty darned snazzy if you ask me. Tom was a small man, 5'7" and 150 lb. He had reddish-brown hair, which was somewhat thinning and that he combed straight back. He worked in the woods, so dressing up was not part of his daily routine. On workdays, I saw him in heavy twill pants, a flannel shirt, a sturdy coat, cork boots, and a tin hat. I would often sit in that hat and rock back and forth in it, just for fun. When he wasn't on the job, he wore neatly pressed pants and a button-up shirt with the sleeves rolled halfway up. To be really stylish, my dad, of course, wore a fedora hat that he tilted to one side. For dress, there was the blue pinstriped suit, and for more casual days, he sported a suede leather jacket. My dad looked like someone who, had his family not moved from Cornwall, England, just before World War I, would have been in the Royal Air Force in World War II.

Irma also knew how to look good. She had lots of salt-and-pepper hair and wore it stylishly short. When she dressed up, Mom wore outfits accessorized with hats and gloves and hose with seams in the back. Although at one time she was a small woman, by the time I was a young girl, she had become somewhat sturdy, shall we say. Mom always blamed Dad for her weight gain. She said that she would have never gained weight if he hadn't had always wanted her to sit down and have coffee and cake with him. Mom was a very good cook, and any woman who could make pasties and cinnamon rolls like she could deserved to grow ample. Nevertheless, Irma liked beautiful clothes. She passed that trait down to me, and I happily accepted. To surprise Mom, Dad often sent my sister Sharon and I to Mildred's Dress Shop in downtown Molalla to pick out a new dress for her. It was great fun for us. He would give us $20 and tell us to buy something nice. Mom did have nice things. I thought she looked great in her wool plaid Pendleton jacket. Even though she was not born of class and style, she had it in her own right.

Tom was a quiet man whose intelligence was apparent. He could build just about anything he set his mind to. Irma was a little more talkative and just as sharp. Mom was always working. She cooked and baked, took care of elderly people, and in the summer, she worked the night shift at the Woodburn cannery. She was ambitious and was willing to put out the energy for her beloved family. Tom, though slight, was strong and wiry, so much so that at one time, he was a bouncer in a roadhouse in

Michigan. In Molalla, he was very good at his job and highly respected in his industry. Both Tom and Irma were well liked in our little community. They were the dependable sort of people that were common in my childhood.

One year a carnival came to our small town. Why, I'm not sure. But everyone wanted to see the big show and ride on the rides. My mom, dad, sister, and I waited in the long line to get in. When it was our turn to purchase the tickets, the total cost for the family was four dollars. Mom and Dad didn't bring that much money with them. They didn't think the entrance cost would be nearly that high. My dad's boss, Bob Hanson, happened to be in line in back of us and loaned Dad the money for us to get in. I think my mother was deeply embarrassed by this event. The next morning, I overheard them discussing the high prices of the carnival and their dismay about not being prepared. But as it was with Tom and Irma, they would not be embarrassed any further. They made sure that Dad had the money in his pocket to immediately repay the loan from his boss. There would be no delay, not even one day in paying it back. What would people think? That was the crux of the fifties for us—working hard, respect, reputation, looking good, feeling even better.

We often look back at our childhood with eyes possibly clouded with impressions of innocence and, sometimes, even awe. But then, how could we not?

CHAPTER
Eleven

Chicken Whisperer

MY PARENTS, TOM AND IRMA Traise, lived in Molalla, Oregon in the 1950s with their three children. Most American homes and lives were not sophisticated, but still full of authenticity and character. There was a sweetness about our existence then.

During much of the Molalla time, the Traises lived in a two-story house on Toliver Road about a mile outside of town. The house was somewhat large with three bedrooms, lots of other rooms, nooks and crannies, and a wood-burning stove to heat the whole place, right in the middle of the house on the first floor. Since my brother Dick was off in the army, my sister Sharon and I each had our own room. When I was little, I think that I sort of roamed around for sleeping purposes because I often ended up sleeping with either my sister or my parents rather than by myself. No one seemed to mind.

We had an acre of property that was wooded. It was a perfect setting for our house, the garage, my dad's workshop, a play area for me, a tetherball spot, and of course, a garden. I especially liked my dad's shop. It was immaculate. Every tool had its place, and everything was kept in order. I spent many hours there just sitting in the corner watching my dad work. Sometimes he would give me a magnet with a long coiled bendable handle to play with. I would play in the sawdust, making trails and designs before he would sweep up.

Tom was quite the carpenter and made a goodly number of our household items in that shop. One year, early in our time at the Molalla house, it snowed heavily on a winter morning. In just no time at all, my dad had made me a sled, and I was careening down the street by our house.

We had animals at our place; some were pets, and other creatures simply got to live on the property with us. We just had the basics: cats, dogs, chickens, and ducks, nothing fancy. I wanted peacocks, but my father would have none of them. He said that peacocks were noisy and obnoxious. So my parents talked me into ducks. We had two, Pat and Mike. They followed me around and quacked, and that was about it. They also left a lot of droppings in the yard, and my parents were not at all happy about that. We were forever stepping in it. We did not make money or food from our animals. They were just around us, and I enjoyed them all.

As I mentioned, the Traises had chickens. Not many, just enough for a few eggs, I think. They were Banties, and I had a favorite hen. I did not name her, but she was very tame, and I would carry her around a lot. I even took her to town once nestled in my arm. Now, you would think that it would not be easy to carry a chicken to town. (I might have been something of a chicken whisperer.) But I did take her to Molalla, and there couldn't have been a more piteous sight than a skinny bucked-tooth young girl with a chicken walking around a small logging town. I'm sure people were saying, "Oh, there goes Tom and Irma's little girl, and my god, she has a chicken under her arm!"

That one time when I was on my chicken trip, I took her to see John and Ida Wright. They were an elderly couple for whom my mother cooked and cleaned. Mrs. Wright was a spry small woman with black hair that she wore under a hairnet. Mr. Wright was almost blind. He sat in one chair most of the time while Mrs. Wright did what she could around the house. Their daughter in California hired my mother because the Wrights had a wood-burning cookstove, and my mom knew how to cook on woodstoves. Mom always told me it wasn't easy to make bread on a wood-burning stove, but by golly, she could do it.

When I took my chicken to see the Wrights, my mother, of course, gave me permission. There was no worry that I couldn't handle it or that people would make fun of me. There was no concern that the Wrights would think that I was odd. It was, after all, a little girl, a chicken, and Molalla. The Wrights were very kind to me when I took my chicken to see them. They were enthusiastic and gracious. I sat in the chair opposite Mr. Wright and chatted with him. We didn't stay long as I saw them several times a week anyway, and my chicken and I soon went home. I think that my Banty left a little something in the chair, and I'm not talking an egg, but Mrs. Wright never mentioned it, and neither did I.

How odd it is to walk to town with a chicken, to sleep at night with various members of your family, to sit and just watch someone work for hours. Today it would seem unusual to find enjoyment in these things. Today it is wonderful to remember.

CHAPTER
Twelve

Molalla

My parents, Tom and Irma Traise, lived in Molalla, Oregon in the 1950s with their three children. America was literally on the move. After the war, people were finding their place again. For a while, we found ours. Molalla is a small logging town in the foothills of the mountain range that borders the great Willamette Valley. The Willamette Valley was the end of the famous Oregon Trail. In the 1850s, thousands of people migrated from the eastern United States to the west via the Oregon Trail. Those brave settlers walked most of the way. The trip took months, and many died along the trail. But Oregon was known as Eden because it was a new start and had all of the timber and fields and promise that the venturesome needed. So it was for Tom and Irma Traise in the 1950s.

Molalla was a town of a few thousand people, give or take. There was a red stoplight at the intersection in the middle of town, and that was it for crowd control. Traffic problems were pretty much nonexistent, except for the logging trucks, of which we needed to be ever mindful. When I was about eight, there was one incident with me and an automobile driver. An older gentleman was turning at the red light, and he didn't see me walking my bike across the intersection. I could see him and the inevitable. I dropped the bike and ran. He drove over my blue bike as I watched. That was pretty exciting stuff then. When my parents were called, Tom was cool, and Irma was frantic. After the whole event was taken care of and I was home, my mom asked me if I wanted to sit on her lap. I said okay and did so. By that time I was pretty old to sit on my mother's lap, but I think doing so was more for her benefit than for mine.

Logging was the main industry in Molalla. And we didn't log spindly little trees; we had huge firs and cedars. Trees cut down were routinely four or more feet across and a hundred feet long. Sometimes the logs were so big that only one or two would fit on a truck. The logs were hauled down from the mountains and milled in Molalla or floated downriver to Portland. The logging companies had their own private roads, and we knew to stay off them. The trucks with their heavy loads would come barreling down the winding roads, and often, there would be no time to stop for anyone. Accidents either in the woods or on the roads were not uncommon.

In reality, however, I could safely walk everywhere, and I did. My mom would send me most Saturday mornings to the bakery to get doughnuts for my dad. (He liked the glazed doughnuts; I preferred the plain cake ones.) I would go to town the back way, down a trail along the railroad tracks. I would also walk to school, to friends' houses, or to visit where my mom was taking care of her old people. No one cared, and no one questioned. It was a safe place, and there were no worries about crazy people attacking or abducting little girls.

Even though there was safety for me, in a sort of oppositional reality, Molalla was a rough-and-tumble place. True to that oppositional existence, there was a church of every faith, and in fact, there were more churches than taverns, but not by many. The White Horse Tavern on Main Street was famous and still is today for its wild and woolly atmosphere. And even though my dad was a bouncer when he was a young man in Michigan, Tom did not frequent the White Horse Tavern. Irma was very clear on that, not that he would have done so anyway.

When my family first moved to Molalla, my mother kept hearing about Ollie Driver. Ollie Driver this, and Ollie Driver that. Don't get caught by Ollie Driver. Better watch out for Ollie Driver. She thought that the Ollie Driver must have been some sort of big piece of logging equipment. Well, Ollie Driver was the name of the one and only policeman in Molalla, Sgt. Ollie Driver. So you know that when the town has only one policeman, and everyone's talking about not getting caught by him, it could only mean one of two things: that no one had respect for him and wasn't worried about being caught, or that everyone had respect for him and was worried about getting caught by him. With my mother, it was just clear that she was clueless in both perspectives.

At the main crossroads where the red stoplight was downtown, the Bentley Feed Co. store stood large on the northwest corner. I loved going in there and would often just stop in to see what was new. The smells of the grains and the animals were so sweet to me. I truly loved it. My favorite time to visit the shop was in the spring when the little chickens filled the warm incubators, and their cheeping was so loud that you could hear them even before you walked in the door. I would stand and look and watch and touch, ever so carefully, those little chickens. All the while the big men clerking at the store would watch me, making sure that I was not hurting any of the babies. I was not.

On the northeast corner of the intersection was the Rexall Drug Store. It was orange and black and had everything we needed in the line of drugs and beauty. We didn't need much. You could go in and sit at the counter and get such treats as a nickel ice cream cone, a root beer float, or an ice cream sundae. I mostly stuck with a small vanilla ice cream cone. At that age, trying new foods was not on my most-fun-things-to-do list.

The little town of Molalla had all the other basic retail shops, garages, and offices, which included this little girl's favorites: the Five-and-Dime Store, Dickinson's Grocery, and the Molalla Bakery. We also had the Man's Shop and Mildred's Dress Shop to make sure that our rustic population was elegantly and properly dressed. There was also the Everhart and Kent Funeral Home, where the funeral directors dressed Tom in his blue pinstriped suit and helped my brother Dick and I plan his funeral.

Tom and Irma Traise lived in Molalla, Oregon in the 1950s with their three children. For me, it was a precious few short years, but Tom and Irma made it worth remembering.

Epilogue

TOM AND IRMA TRAISE MOVED to Molalla, Oregon in 1953 with their three children. True to their hardworking nature and entrepreneurial spirit, they bought a small bakery in a neighboring city late in that decade. It was called Mom's Doughnut Shop. Irma ran the bakery, and Tom maintained his job in the woods for Weyerhaeuser Timber Company. The family moved from Molalla in 1960. In May of 1963, the DC 10 Caterpillar bulldozer that Tom was driving rolled backward off a cliff. He fell out of the huge machine on the way down, and the DC 10 landed on top of him. Tom died instantly. Irma left us in a far less dramatic way. She continued working her whole life, but in May 1987, Irma simply sat down on a chair and departed from this earth. She too died instantly. She, in fact, looked so good sitting on the chair that the older woman she was caring for could not tell whether Irma was actually gone or not.

Comments from around the world about Tom and Irma~Chronicles of the 1950s.

We have been enjoying your poems since you first made your debut on Radio Kinver, our English is fairly good but we wanted to say how much we really enjoy your series of memory slices called 'Tom and Irma'.

They show us how very similar we are in spite of national and cultural differences. We hear you and memories of our own mothers and fathers rise up in us too and clearer glances do we gain. You have so deep a connection to people through your writing and we salute your talent and great gifts.

Sasha and Alexis
Novgorod Republic

* * * * * * * * *

Susan Patterson, I salute you and your simple sounding yet really deep and complex writing. You write so very well and achieve that elegant simplicity that hides the true art. Thank you for all the delights you give us week by week, a true international talent as well as a very sharing one.

Josh
Calgary, Canada

* * * * * * * * *

Susan Patterson has the rare knack of constructing simple lines and few words, which contrive to slip under the most careful guard and penetrate our souls and leave their wisdom for us to relish. The 'Tom and Irma' ones are different and yet even more deep. It is so good to find a writer who has reinvented the art of the parable for modern times.

Deborah
Lecturer (retired)
English Language and Literature
Birkbeck College, London

* * * * * * * * *

When I first heard one of the Susan Patterson's 'Tom and Irma' works I was taken aback, how could such a short work be so effective and draw such strong feelings from me. As each work followed with its laughter and tears I realised that the magic of these works is the same as in her tea poems. Knowing what she wants to say and then compressing it in the minimal number of words. I feel that the poems were the parents of the 'T&I' works; it may not have been possible one without other. May Ms. Patterson know our on going joy and delight at all her works may they both march on side by side for a long time to come to give us continued pleasure.

Margaret
Lecturer
Girton College, Cambridge

* * * * * * * * *

Wow, now you know we have loved these since the get-go and we treasure them with their clear focus and deep honesty, but to hear them in order is to realise what a treasure is there. I hope Susan knows how important her work in this respect is. We love all her work and find it so vital and comforting and surprising too but in 'T&I' she reconnects us to our own roots and shows us how to understand our past.

Please tell Susan that she is a vital part of the world's culture and of the USA's legacy of truth. We salute her with our admiration and our respectful love.

Kenny and Merrily
Wichita, Kansas

* * * * * * * * *

Now to 'Tom and Irma' I was at first startled then seduced and now I long for each new episode. She has mixed 'Golden Eisenhower Age' nostalgia with the sharp focus of a child's memories and the brilliant retrospective learning of the adult. Rare qualities indeed, please tell Earlene from me a Southerner that she is one Yankee I admire and value greatly. Thank You Susan Patterson .

Howard
New York
(originally from Atlanta)